First Facts®

How Bees Make Honey

the BIG PICTURE

CAPSTONE PRESS
a capstone imprint

Louise Spilsbury

First Facts is published by Capstone Press, a Capstone imprint,
151 Good Counsel Drive, P.O. Box 669, Mankato, Minnesota 56002.
www.capstonepub.com

First published in 2010 by A&C Black Publishers Limited, 36 Soho Square, London W1D 3QY
www.acblack.com

Produced for A&C Black by Calcium. www.calciumcreative.co.uk

042010
005769ACS11

Library of Congress Cataloging-in-Publication Data
Spilsbury, Louise.
  How Bees Make Honey / by Louise Spilsbury.
      p. cm. — (First facts, the big picture)
  Includes index.
  ISBN 978-1-4296-5535-4 (library binding)
  ISBN 978-1-4296-5536-1 (paperback)
  1. Honeybee—Juvenile literature. 2. Honey—Juvenile literature.
  I. Title. II. Series.

  QL568.A6S766 2011
  595.79'9—dc22   2010008901

Every effort has been made to trace copyright holders and to obtain their permission for use of copyright material.

This book is produced using paper that is made from wood grown in managed, sustainable forests. It is natural,
renewable and recyclable. The logging and manufacturing processes conform to the environmental regulations
of the country of origin.

Acknowledgements

The publishers would like to thank the following for their kind permission to reproduce their photographs:

Cover: Shutterstock: Tischenko Irina (front), Alle (back). **Pages:** Shutterstock: Takiev Alexander 23, Alle 15, Anyka
11, Ason 6–7, Nikola Bilic 14, Katrina Brown 8, 16, Chas 13, Steve Cukrov 7, Nikolay Stefanov Dimitrov 16–17,
Dimos 22–23, Tomo Jesenicnik 10, Kirsanov 17, Joanna Zopoth-Lipiejko 3, Manfredxy 4–5, Dave Massey
2–3, Zacarias Pereira da Mata 1, MilousSK 12, Fedorov Oleksiy 8–9, 14–15, Photoslb.com 9, Pixinity 12–13,
Marianna Raszkowska 20–21, Vladimir Sazonov 4–5, Bruce T. Smith 18–19, Suravid 10–11, Filipe B.
Varela 24, Kulish Viktoria 19, WDG Photo 18, Yaroslav 21.

Contents

Honey Menu

Bees are amazing. They make honey that they can eat, and we can eat it too!

Honeybees

There are many kinds of bees, but honeybees make the most honey. They live all over the world.

Bees make honey to eat in winter.

Don't touch!

Bees look beautiful, but beware! The yellow and black stripes on their bodies are a warning. If you touch a bee, it might sting you.

Hands off!

Honeybee Homes

Honeybees live together in nests. Some nests are small, but some are very big.

Making nests

Bees make nests in all sorts of places. They make nests on trees and bushes, in caves, and on cliffs.

Home sweet home

Busy bees

Nests are busy places! Bees make and store all their honey in their nests.

This bee nest hangs from a tree.

Inside a Nest

Inside a honeybee nest there are many little cells. These are like tiny rooms where young bees live and honey is stored.

Same shape, same size

The cells are all the same shape and size. Each cell has six sides, so they fit together neatly to form a **honeycomb**.

I'm buzzy working!

8

Wax works

Bees make cells from **wax**. To make wax, bees mix **fat** from their stomachs with spit from their mouths.

Bees take away dirt, poop, and old food to keep the nest clean.

9

Teamwork

Bees in a nest work as a team. Different bees do different jobs.

Queen in charge!

The queen bee lays the eggs. Male bees called drones **mate** with the queen so she can lay eggs. Worker bees collect and make food. They also care for the eggs and young bees.

Every bee has a job to do.

Killer bees

Killer bees make a lot of honey, but hundreds of them attack at once if their nest is in danger!

Buzz off!

11

Honey Recipe

Honeybees need nectar to make honey. Nectar is a sweet juice found in flowers.

Busy bees

Worker honeybees suck up the nectar through their tongues. They carry the nectar back to the nest in a special part of their body.

A bee uses its tongue like a drinking straw!

Dance with me!

Honeybees tell each other where to find flowers by dancing! They walk in a wiggly line to show other bees which way to go.

This way!

Making Honey

Worker bees feed some nectar to the bees that stay behind in the nest. They use the rest of the nectar to make honey.

Spit and mix!

Honeybees mix nectar with juices in their mouths. They put drops of this mixture into the honeycomb cells. They fan it with their wings to dry it.

Runny honey!

Honey is the sticky mixture bees put inside cells.

Honey stores

In winter, the flowers on most plants die. Without flowers, there is no nectar for bees to make honey. Bees put wax lids on honey cells to keep their honey fresh.

Honey For Us

We get our honey from beehives. These are nests that **beekeepers** build for bees to make honey in.

Enough for bees, too

When honey in a hive is ready, beekeepers lift out the honeycombs. They scrape the wax lids off the cells and take out the honey. They then put it in jars.

Hey!

Take care!

Bees get angry if people touch their nest. This is why beekeepers wear clothes and hats that cover their body and face.

This honeycomb is full of honey.

17

Different Honey

The taste and smell of a honey depends on the kind of flowers the nectar came from.

Honey flavors

Eucalyptus trees grow mainly in Australia, so that is where most eucalyptus honey comes from. Heather grows well in Scotland, so that is where most heather-flavored honey comes from.

Sunflower honey from France is thick and yellow!

Honey time

In warm places such as Africa, there are flowers all year round. This means bees make honey here for most of the year.

Awesome Bees

Bees are awesome. As well as making honey that we can eat, they help plants to grow!

Bee gardeners!

When a bee visits a flower, it rubs its body against the **pollen** on the flower. When the bee lands on another flower, some of this pollen rubs onto the new flower. Pollen helps the new flower make **seeds**. New plants can grow from the seeds.

Help!

A bee may visit 100 flowers in just one trip!

Bees in trouble

Some bees are dying because people are cutting down trees, so there are fewer places for bee nests.

Pollen

Glossary

beekeepers people who keep hives of bees

fat thick substance stored in an animal's body

honeycomb set or group of six-sided cells that bees build from wax

mate something animals do to make babies

nectar sweet, sugary substance found in the center of a flower's petals

nest place an animal builds to live in

pollen powder from a flower that can make other flowers grow seeds

seeds seeds are made inside flowers. Seeds can grow into new plants.

wax stuff that bees make in their bodies. Bees use wax to make the cells in a honeycomb.

Further Reading

FactHound offers a safe, fun way to find Internet sites related to this book. All of the sites on FactHound have been researched by our staff.

Here's all you do:

Visit www.facthound.com

FactHound will fetch the best sites for you!

Books

Honey Bees (Blastoff! Readers: World of Insects) by Colleen Sexton, Bellwether Media (2007).

Honey (Food) by Louise Spilsbury, Heinemann (2001).

How do Bees Make Honey? (Tell Me Why, Tell Me How) by Melissa Stewart, Marshall Cavendish Benchmark (2009).

Index